To Kathy

Jennifer Mary

The Breath of God

Is it really a choice?

by
Jennifer Mary

"The Lord God formed man from the dust of the ground and breathed into his nostrils the breath of life and man became a living being."
Genesis 2:7

xulon
PRESS

The Breath of God
Is it really a choice?
by Jennifer Mary

Printed in the United States of America

ISBN 9781613797228

www.xulonpress.com

DEDICATION

T his book is dedicated to God, my husband Ben, my four daughters who are my "Girlie Pearlies," and their children, their Pearls.

"In the fifth month of pregnancy: The amniotic fluid helps your baby develop his/her lungs, while in the womb your baby practices breathing by breathing in and out the water in the amniotic sac. The baby swallows and inhales the amniotic fluid and replaces the volume in the amniotic sac by urinating and exhaling the liquid."

— **http://www.babiesonline.com**

Introduction

My name is Jennifer Mary, and I was born in 1961. Although I had three older sisters, my mother said that when I was born she realized that babies were a miracle from God; I always felt special knowing that. My brother Joe was born two years after me. When the five of us were young, we lived in a pink house in a town south of Boston, Massachusetts. My dad worked as head chef at a local restaurant, and my mom was a homemaker. We went to a Catholic Church, and we did not believe in abortion. But while it's a terribly heavy burden for a young person to make a life-and-death decision, whether to abort the baby in my womb was the decision I faced at age 16.

On January 22, 1973, when I was 11, abortion became legal in America. There are now 1.2 million every year in the United States, and a total of 52 million since the passing of *Roe v. Wade*. Today, it is legal in many states for a teen to get an abortion without her parents' consent, and it has become clear that people have been using abortion as birth control. Part of the problem is a lack of information: these young girls and women are not told at abortion clinics that a baby's heart begins beating in the womb at 22 days after conception. Though eyes, legs, and hands are forming during week five,* a pregnant woman is told that the baby growing inside her is just a blob.

Many girls I've known believed this lie and had abortions. I nearly did myself; only by the grace of God was I saved from ending my teen pregnancy. Although I don't like to read or write (I struggled at school and have A.D.D.), 31 years later I feel the Lord calling me to tell my story in the hope of saving other babies. So the first two parts of this volume present the story of how I chose life for my daughter Sarah and the testimonies of Sarah and her family about how this decision blessed their lives. Next are the personal stories of women who have had abortions and men whose partners had abortions, and the pain they still experience today – except for a 22-year-old woman named Laura, who died having an abortion. The book ends with an exhortation to choose life, an encouragement to seek healing from the pain of abortion through Jesus Christ, and an unusual opportunity called "The Breath of God" that will promote personal healing. Even if you don't read every page in this book, I hope you will read this final section.

Some who read this may be surprised when I speak of getting a "word" from the Lord or saying, "The Lord told me ...." But the Scriptures tell us that when a person comes to faith in Jesus Christ, the Holy Spirit comes to live inside her or him, acting as Counselor and guide in a very personal way: "But if the Spirit of Him who raised Jesus from the dead dwells in you, He who raised Christ Jesus from the dead will also give life to your mortal bodies through His Spirit who dwells in you." (Rom. 8:11; NIV) What I describe is not unusual, but part of the amazing privilege of a close faith walk with Jesus.

Here is my story, and the story of Sarah.

* Statistics taken from the National Right to Life website, <u>www. nrlc.org</u>.

A TRIP TO MAUI

In September 2007 my husband Ben and I traveled to Maui, Hawaii to meet our new grandson, Benjamin Keawe Rex. What a name! When our daughter Sarah was trying to think what to call him, the name Benjamin, which means "Son of My Right Hand", kept coming to her. She already liked the name Keawe, meaning "Southern Star" in Hawaiian, and her Hawaiian-born husband TD liked Rex. But Sarah's friends would always pat her pregnant belly and say, "Hi, Benjamin." Also, her father-in-law had made a wooden car for the coming baby and carved the name Ben into it. So Benjamin Keawe Rex he was, the name planned for him by God.

I could hardly wait to see Sarah, her husband, and their little daughter Nalani Rose, too — it had been a long time. Two weeks earlier, Sarah had called to say she was in labor. But when they went to the hospital two hours away, she wasn't quite ready to be admitted. They had to go stay with friends nearby, until the baby was finally born on September 15 – my birthday. Sarah told me she thought he'd waited on purpose.

We were still about five hours away when suddenly I felt God was speaking to me. One stormy night in November 1977, when I was pregnant with Sarah, the Lord had impressed on me a "word" from Psalm 78:6 that mentions *"...their sons yet to be born."* Now, on the plane, I felt God saying to me, *"This is the son I was talking about in 1977."* I already had two grandsons from my other daughters. But Sarah was the child in my womb at that time and I began to cry, to think I almost ended her life. She has been such a blessing to Ben and me, as has her beautiful family in Maui. Now a grandson whose God-inspired name matched that of his grandfather had been born on my birthday. I saw clearly that God had planned it all and was overwhelmed with thankfulness.

But it almost didn't happen.

THE MOVE

It was going to be a fresh start for me. I had lived on Cape Cod for ten years from the age of five, when my mom told us we were moving. I'd never heard of the new town, and thought it a strange name. *Marshfield?* But my dad had been offered the position of head chef at a restaurant in nearby Pembroke; they'd promised more money and fewer hours, plus bonuses. Despite that, he would be on the job six days a week from seven A.M. until ten P.M.; I didn't really have a relationship with him because he was never home. But he was a good man, although rather strict in his discipline.

On Cape Cod I'd had a tomboy childhood, especially during the summers. Our family went to the Catholic Church on Sundays, but on weekdays my siblings and I would go to the beach, play baseball and tag with neighbors, then ride our banana-seat bikes until the street lights came on. We caught fish with our bare hands at the herring run, walked to the penny candy store to spend our 50-cent allowances, and on our way home cut through the woods to see how far we could jump the stream. I loved to run and jump and run around barefoot, and my brother Joe and I often played Hogan's Heroes in our backyard with a big flashlight.

But all that was over now: I was growing up, and there was going to be a new me in this place called Marshfield. I was a little scared to be leaving my beloved Cape Cod Tech, the high school I'd attended freshman year and where I'd first thought of becoming a graphic artist. I'd struggled in school for years, even staying back in kindergarten because they didn't feel I was ready for first grade. So all my friends had always been a year ahead of me. After summer school, visits to a psychologist, a brief stint on Ritalin, and Special Ed classes, my self-esteem was low to the point where I felt stupid – though I'd enjoyed the one-on-one attention from my mom as we visited the psychologist and went for ice cream afterwards. Now I wondered miserably if I'd be able to succeed academically at this new high school.

But the real reason I was ready for a change had nothing to do with schoolwork. Several boys on the Cape had coerced me to have sex, and because they were my boyfriends I thought it was their right. The first one literally took me into a field and pressured me until I gave in. At first, I said no; at 14, all I wanted was to kiss a boy. But I'd always been told "Be quiet" and "Be good," and had never learned to express my feelings or make my wishes known. My trials at school and the A.D.D. diagnosis certainly hadn't helped.

It seems incredible to me now, but I stayed with that boyfriend for a full year after he first had sex with me. (I cannot say we ever had sex with each other.) Then he broke up with me, and a year or so later I started dating a musician. But he wanted sex right away as well, and again I found myself saying "no" to a man to no avail. The night that happened I was devastated, and terribly upset with myself for letting it happen again. Early the next morning I left the house where we'd rendezvoused (supposedly for a night of playing music) and rode my bike a very long way home, crying all the way. I'd lied to my mother about where I was going, and the whole episode was so traumatizing that I broke up with this man the next time I saw him. I was relieved to be out of that.

Both of these boyfriends would later do jail time, one for rape. But my third boyfriend was an improvement; we actually had a relationship where we enjoyed going to the beach and doing other things before the sex started. But when he wanted sex as well I just let him go ahead, thinking that this must be what everyone was doing. But inside, I knew it was wrong, and that relationship only lasted a month or so before I learned we were moving.

Given these terrible experiences and the pattern I'd allowed myself to get into, I was glad and excited to make a change. Right before we moved I made a pact with my sister Melinda, who was just one year older than I, that neither of us would have sex until we were married. Although it did not occur to me then, today I can understand and appreciate how God protected me by not letting me get pregnant by any of those boys.

I loved our new home in Marshfield. We'd never had a dining room or a fireplace with a mantle. My mom, a talented decorator, bought pretty country furniture with matching curtains for the living room. Outside, lush grass grew in the yard — the Cape soil had been too sandy for a decent lawn — and the trees had green leaves instead of ugly old pine needles. When I woke in the mornings, I could hear beautiful birdsong, instead of the cawing of black crows and bluejays on the Cape. I tried to whistle the tunes and did pretty well. Even the sun seemed brighter in Marshfield; I felt a little rich.

Then one day my mom took Melinda and me shopping for summer clothes: we bought cute tank tops, shorts and sun dresses. We both have a slender build, and I would pull up a little of my wavy hair from the sides to make a ponytail.

It was the summer of 1977, and the "new me" was ready for some fun.

THE BOYS

Melinda and I invited her friend Diane from the Cape to spend the weekend. A slender girl with black curly hair, Diane always made us laugh. We were cleaning the house and went out front to shake the tablecloth. Some boys across the street called out, "Hey! What are you doing?" We ran back into the house, laughing, and soon heard a knock at the front door. Because my mother wasn't home we scooted under the dining room table. But then we crawled out, peeked out the window, and saw some cute boys. We decided, giggling, that it was safe to answer the door.

We introduced ourselves: Melinda, Jenny, our friend Diane. One of the boys was Ricky, the other Ben. Ricky had a big smile and laughed a lot; he was good-looking, and living at Ben's house because he and his mom were not getting along. But I liked Ben, who was cute with curly, dark brown hair that peeped from under his grey hat that had a black ribbon around it. He had a nice smile and was tall and thin, wearing cut-off jeans and a brown-flowered shirt. He seemed so cool.

There were many kids our age in the neighborhood, and soon a lot of boys began to stop at our house. It was fun getting all that attention. One day as Melinda and I walked home from the center of town, we saw Ben driving towards us in a blue station wagon. We put out our thumbs, and he stopped and told us to jump in the back window since he had friends with him. (I didn't realize the danger of thumbing even just around town, although that day we did know Ben.) He drove us home and called "See you around!" as we jumped out of the car. I hoped he meant it, and he must have; after that he and Ricky started calling us and stopping by.

THE NEVER-ENDING SUMMER

It was the Fourth of July, and Ben and I were on the beach in Marshfield watching the fireworks. Many bonfires were burning up and down the beach, and some people had brought their own fireworks. Staring up into the beautiful night sky, we got into a long conversation about God and agreed we both believed in Him. That night Ben kissed me for the first time, and we officially began dating. Melinda and Ricky became a couple, as well.

What a summer it was! Ben, Rick, Melinda, and I were always together. At beach parties we built bonfires, ate goodies, and drank soda and beer. We also went out to the private end of Duxbury Beach, where a friend's family had a house. You needed a four-wheel drive to get there, and the guys would drive so fast that our heads would hit the ceiling of the car. We played football in the rain, getting all muddy. Other times we'd go to pool parties or just go for pizza, ice cream, or late-night Chinese food. A bunch of us might also go to the drive-in; it was about $5 a carload, and we'd even cram people into the trunk. And if there wasn't anything going on, we'd just drive about just looking for friends or a party. Ben always had music playing in his station wagon: Led Zeppelin, Aerosmith, Lynyrd Skynyrd. And when the Marshfield Fair started in August we snuck in almost every night, just walking around eating fried dough and playing a few games.

I also spent time at Ben's house. It was old, but I liked its old-fashioned character and homeyness. Ben lived with his mom, dad and three sisters. His mom, Jan, was a Christian who welcomed me warmly and always had a delicious, homemade cake for us to snack on. They had a small pond out back, so we'd go fishing in their rowboat; in the winter, we skated on the ice.

Some nights, Melinda and I stayed up late watching movies in our living room. Around midnight, we would sneak out the window to meet Ricky and Ben, who'd done the same and walked about two miles to our house through the woods. We'd go to the new houses that were being built behind our house; they didn't even have windows or doors yet. I remember singing Beatles songs as we tramped down the new roads. We would go into a house to make out, and knew we had to go home when we heard the neighbors' rooster crow because my dad would be getting up soon. It would be disastrous to run into him.

It was around this time that Ben and I first had sex. My mom had given me "the talk" when I was around 13, after I got my period. She'd been told sex was bad until you are married, but her mother never talked to her about it. She didn't want Melinda and me to grow up feeling that way, so had told us, "Do not have sex until you are in love and know you will marry that person."

But at 15, I felt I was falling in love with Ben. He was a gentleman, who would open the car door for me and even light my cigarettes. I'd never been with a boy like that, and enjoyed being treated as if I were special. When we drove together I could snuggle up against him without feeling he was pressuring me to be physical. We didn't plan to have sex; actually we had discussed how it would be better not to. But then it happened anyway, gradually and slowly. But this time I didn't mind. My dad had only expressed his love for all of us through working too hard and disciplining us; with Ben, I finally felt loved. Later I would wish I'd said no, and saved myself for my husband-to-be. But if you'd asked me then, I'd have said 1977 was the best summer of my life.

I didn't know it was the last summer I'd be carefree.

SCHOOL STARTS

September came and school started; I was now in tenth grade. Despite my apprehensions, I soon had a lot of friends among the geeks, smart kids, and jocks. But mostly I hung out with the freaks, who were smart but acted like they thought they were cool. The guys had long hair and we all wore baggy clothes, smoked weed, and did other drugs. We pretended we didn't care about school, and didn't do sports. Looking back, I wish I had, especially track. I now see that what I did wasn't cool at all; I was just passing through, hanging with the wrong crowd. Outside of school, though, I was still seeing Ben, who had similar friends in his own grade.

I was also interested in astrology. I read some books about it, and used to ask people what their sign was. I thought astrological signs had to do with believing in God, but Ben came to my house one day and told me that God doesn't want anyone to look to astrology for the answers in life. I was surprised. He told me to get my Bible and showed me Isaiah 47:13-14, which says that astrologers were like stubble that would be burned up; they would not be able to save themselves.

I realized that Ben really did have a Christian upbringing, thanks to his mom, and that what he was saying about God's view of astrology was correct. I threw away my astrology books, because I believed in God and wanted to do what was right. At 15, of course I was aware that my parents wouldn't be pleased by what I was doing with Ben physically, but even at this point I didn't think to consider what God's Word said about it.

One day in October, Ben called and said he was grounded. I rode my bike to his house, and we met in the woods across the street. I really felt I was falling in love with him; he seemed to like me a lot, continued to treat me well, and I enjoyed the attention. But Ben didn't have or use protection that day, and I believe this is when I got pregnant. I'd always let him take care of birth control because I had no way to get the Pill and knew nothing about other options. I was scared afterwards, because we both knew we'd taken a risk, and thought back to the last day of my period. It was the middle of my cycle, the time when you can get pregnant. I waited for my period, but it didn't come; I waited a few more days. By the time I was eight days late, I was feeling sick in the mornings and knew this was a bad sign. Somehow I obtained a pregnancy test and took it, and couldn't believe my eyes: I was pregnant!

I had turned 16 a month earlier. *What am I going to do now?* I thought. I knew I had to tell Ben, but first I told my sister Melinda. She was shocked, although she couldn't be too angry with me because she had just run away from home to live with her boyfriend. Obviously we had both broken our pact not to have sex until we were married. But I hadn't been worrying about it, because I knew I loved Ben. My parents were terribly upset about Melinda, and things were very stressful at our house.

I then called Ben and told him the news. He was shocked too and said, "You have to get an abortion. We can't have a baby!" I told him I couldn't have an abortion, as it kills babies. We talked for days about what to do, and cried together a lot. Neither of us blamed the other, but Ben was upset because he felt this meant the end to his plans for his life, not to mention his teenaged freedom. I reasoned that I couldn't tell my parents, as they were already upset about my sister. I thought my dad would literally have a heart attack if he knew I'd had sex and was pregnant. I was afraid and confused.

I knew I loved Ben, but now he told me he wasn't sure if he loved me. It broke my heart to hear that. I'd been sure he loved me; he was sweet to me, and told me I was funny and cute. But maybe he'd just said those things for one reason. I wished I hadn't given in again! Why hadn't I saved myself for my husband-to-be? *WHY?*

19

We knew I could get an abortion without my parents' consent. But it was an awful thing to do, and I struggled with it terribly. I'd seen a book a friend had on abortion, that showed dead babies in a trash can. Another friend had had an abortion and told me she would never forget the baby's predicted date of birth. I never wanted to feel that way, but finally we decided abortion was our only choice. We couldn't see how we could raise a child – but even worse, I was scared to death of telling my parents. I couldn't imagine what sort of punishment my disciplinarian father would come up with; he would ground my sisters and me for a month for much less serious offenses.

In the middle of all this, Ben called and said his friend Jimmy would give us a ride to a Boston clinic for a "checkup". I agreed, not realizing he meant an abortion. He said later he'd thought he told me, but I didn't hear him. So we skipped classes that day and waited for Jimmy in the rain, in front of the school. But he never showed up. We never knew why, but I realized later that if we'd gone to the clinic, I might have gone through with an abortion. I would have felt trapped, unable to withstand the pressure to complete the plan made without my knowledge. Today, as I look back on that day, I realize that God had protected me yet again from the consequences of a decision that would have caused me pain and ended that of my child.

GOD SPEAKS

I continued to feel sick every day, and we talked more about how I had to have an abortion. Then one weekend Melinda and I visited my friend Melody on the Cape. I told Melody I was pregnant, and she told her mom. Then her mother told my mom, so when my mom came to pick me up she asked me if I was pregnant. I was shocked, and at first said no. But then I began to cry and admitted, "Yes, I am." My mom began to cry, too. I lied and told her I only "did it" once, and she said through her tears, "That's all it takes."

It was a long ride home. I told her that Ben wanted me to get an abortion. She said, "We need to think about that," as if it were a real possibility. I was shocked and couldn't believe my ears. When I got home, I was so confused that I went up to my room in tears. What about our Catholic belief that abortion was wrong? I'd never dreamed I could hear those words from my mother. Now I remembered that Ben's mother Jan had told me that God can speak to you through the Bible, so I brought our big, gold-embossed family Bible to my room. I'd never seen anyone look at it, although our names were all written carefully on the Family Record page at the beginning.

As I sat on my bed sobbing, I felt sick inside and knew for the first time that I absolutely did not want to abort my baby. I cried out to God for help, believing that He was real and that if anyone could help me, it was God. Unknowingly, I opened the Bible to Psalm 77 and read: *"Aloud to God I cry, aloud to God to hear me. On the day of my distress I seek the Lord, by night my hands are stretched out."*

Kneeling on the wood floor and crying, I stretched out my hands before me and continued to read: *"My soul refuses comfort, when I remember God I moan; when I ponder my soul grows faint."*
I read on.

"The waters saw you O God, waters saw you and shuttered, the very depths were troubled. The clouds poured down water, the skies gave forth their voice; your arrows also sped abroad. Your thunder resounded in the whirlwinds, your lighting illumined the world, and the earth quivered and quaked."

When I read those words, it started thundering and lightning outside. I couldn't believe it. I felt the Lord could hear me – that He was right there! I cried even more and asked God what I should do. Should I have an abortion? I read on to Psalm 78:6:

"So that generations to come might know their sons yet to be born, that they too may rise and declare to their sons, that they should put their hope in God, and not forget the deeds of God but keep his commands and not be like their fathers, a generation wayward and rebellious, a generation that kept not its heart steadfast, nor its spirit faithful toward God."

My eyes fell right on *"their sons yet to be born."* I believed then, and believe now, that God was saying to me that I had to have this baby — there were sons yet to be born. I had my answer.
I told my mom I was going to have the baby even if I had to live in the streets. She agreed I shouldn't abort, and admitted she didn't believe in it; she'd just gotten scared. She told me I would have to tell my dad and grandmother. It was hard, but I decided to write each of them a letter. Then I called Ben and told him I was going to have the baby because my mom had found out, and God had told me to have it. He wasn't happy, and still tried to convince me to have an abortion. We had many discussions, but every time I said, "No." Somehow, because I knew God had spoken to me, I was able to be firmer over this than I'd been about having sex in the first place. Even if it meant Ben might leave me.

After this I felt closer to God and would go and pray on a small hill near my house, thinking it would bring me even closer to Him. As I prayed, I remembered that when I was a child I would go into my parents' bedroom to look at the cross of Jesus, the statue of Mary, and my mom's rosary beads. And when I was around 10, I'd dreamed I saw Jesus at the top of a staircase in the sky with an open door. My sister woke me up that night because I was talking in my sleep, saying "God, God." But even though I'd learned the Lord's Prayer at church, I'd never understood how to invite Him into my heart.

I was too ashamed and afraid to speak with my dad and grandmother directly. So I wrote a note to my dad, telling him about my pregnancy, and put it on his pillow. Then I wrote and mailed a letter to my only grandmother, who lived several towns away. I would later learn that my mother removed my father's letter from the pillow until they'd been to a party and she was sure he was in a good mood. I never knew exactly when he received it, because I saw him so little, but meanwhile my grandmother wrote back:

Dear Jenny,

I was quite overwhelmed about your news. I'm sorry it has to be like this as your responsibilities will be so great for one so young. Wish things could have been different. You said you needed for me to understand; Of course you have my love and understanding. I have built the idea in my mind you would really go places as you got older as I think you are very talented. You know these old grandmothers want the best in life for their grandchildren.

I love you too,
Your Grandmother   See you Sunday

I was thrilled to know my grandmother wasn't going to judge me. She would continue to show her love for me throughout my pregnancy and beyond.

PARENTS

A few days after that, Ben and I had to meet with all four of our parents. It was scary, facing Ben's mother and father, and my own father and I still hadn't talked about my pregnancy. All I remember is Ben's parents yelling and my dad saying, "Are you stupid? Didn't you use protection?" After that meeting, I felt as if my dad was angry with me for a week straight; he would give me terrible looks. I felt ashamed and guilty; how could I have done this to my parents? I tried harder now to be a good daughter, and listened to my mom when she told me I had to let Ben go. "If he loves you," she told me, "he will come back." So I tearfully told Ben I wasn't allowed to see him any more. That seemed okay with him; Ben wasn't sure if he loved me anyway. I patted my belly and told the baby we could make it without him.

I felt so alone. My sister had run away, and now it seemed my brother Joe hated me; he got mad one day and told me he was too young to be an uncle. He was 14. I felt so bad, I went to my room and cried. I never would have thought that my actions could affect my family this way.

My mother brought me to her obstetrician for a check-up. The pregnancy test was positive, and although my mom didn't believe in abortion she asked the doctor about it. He got angry, saying he didn't perform abortions, and sent us to an agency. A woman there said I had three choices: to have and keep the baby, give him or her up for adoption, or abort. We were already thinking I'd keep the baby, but the woman told me I couldn't care for one and should give up my child for adoption. That upset my mom, so we left. My mother later told the doctor what they'd said, and he said he would never send anyone there again. He also told her, "When your daughter has the baby, it will be your baby — not hers." I think he thought that because I was so young. But he was wrong.

The baby was due the Fourth of July, one year from the day Ben and I started dating. My parents still weren't sure if they should stand by me to keep the baby or encourage me to give it up. My mom was also afraid of what the neighbors would think, or what people would say if we ran into them in the grocery store. She and my father thought about sending me to a school for pregnant teens in New Hampshire; I was willing to go but scared, and ultimately they didn't send me. Some people did say things: one of my mother's friends told her she was too old to raise a baby (at 41), and another expressed the opinion that I should have an abortion. My answer was, "What if this is the only child I can have?" I knew my parents were ashamed, but I just had to ignore people like that and move on.

Going to school was especially hard. Not many people knew, but I'm sure word got around. I wasn't showing yet, so I didn't talk about it. I was in a new school, the new kid in town, and now I was pregnant. What a mess; my world was falling apart. My mom said I could quit school, but after all my years of struggle I was not going to give up now. Meanwhile, my mom had a counselor come to the house, but after awhile I told her I didn't need it and the counselor came just to talk to her.

Alone a lot, I wrote some poems.

"My life hasn't ended, it's just begun. Don't ruin the present worrying about the past, for there is the future.
I have a new feeling I've never felt before and I'm going to keep it.
I know I'm only young but I can still have some fun with our beautiful baby that is going to come.
Our baby; you're going to be a man someday but today is not the day!
My love, you're only seventeen and you still have some years; but if you marry me you won't be free.
You need someone you can love and that someone is not me.

I'm sixteen, carrying your baby. I will bring this baby up till it doesn't need me. Between now and then maybe you will find the one that you can hold and love, and I pray that someone will be me!
I need you like the flower needs the rain and sun.
I'm not going to cry, I'm going to try!"

My mother also found a poem in a magazine that spoke to her:

"You look at her eyes and her dark smooth hair, and her arms that have held you so tight.
You look at your child, this work of your love, and vow you'll change wrong from right.
You think of the years you've had her to love, though you know it's only fifteen,
You think of the times, good and bad, and how much they've all come to mean.
You think of the flowers she's made quietly in the night, you think of the love notes she's left for you to find in the morning light.
You feel hatred seeping into your heart for the one who hurt your little girl,
You know you can't let this happen; you must go on polishing your precious pearl.
Still you must find an answer and find it right now, while still hanging on by a glove,
and then there it is, the answer is there, as if it had dropped from above.
This is only my baby having a baby; it will be another for me to love!"

I don't know who wrote that poem, but it gave my mom comfort.

THE BLIZZARD OF '78

I woke up on February 6, 1978, four months pregnant and freezing cold. I flicked a switch, and the lights didn't work; I realized the heat was off, looked out the window, and saw a lot of snow. I went to my parents' room to tell them we had no power, but my mom told me my dad was at the restaurant where he now worked in Braintree, feeding masses of people stuck on Route 128. It was the Blizzard of '78.

Facing the storm at home were my mom, my sister Melinda (who'd broken up with her boyfriend and returned), and my brother Joe. The house was below 50 degrees, and I was suffering with a bad cold. Unprepared for a blizzard, we went in the cellar to see what we could burn. We found some crates; then Joe hauled in tree branches from outside and we put up sheets in the doorways to keep the heat in the room. We pushed the couches and chair close to the fireplace, the only warm spot in the house; our backs still felt cold. There was no hot water for showers, and we washed our hands with freezing water.

Suddenly I felt a little flutter in my belly. I told my mom, and she said it must be the baby moving. This was exciting, and as I ate the (gross) spam and eggs my mom cooked in the fireplace I wondered how big the baby inside me actually was. I'd been feeling fat.

We were just starting to think about what else we could burn when we heard a knock on our door. It was Ben, with an armful of wood. As he came in we looked at each other and said hi. He told us how he'd driven to the ocean and seen all the devastation there and the lobster traps washed up on land. Ben's family was okay; they had a wood stove and gas hot water and kitchen stove at their house. It was so good to see Ben. I missed him a lot, and I hoped he missed me.

On the fourth day of the blizzard, my brother's friend Brian and his family invited us over for some warmth and a hot meal. Although Melinda and Joe had walked to the town center to get milk, bread, and a few other things, we hadn't had a real dinner in days. But I felt so dirty. No shower for days, the smell of smoke in my hair and clothes, and I was starting to show. Being 16 and pregnant, I was very embarrassed, though I was pretty sure they knew of my pregnancy. And it was nice of Brian's family to invite us and wonderful to be warm.

Finally we got our electricity back, and I was so thankful. The Blizzard of '78 seemed a lot longer than five days to us, and my parents always made sure to have wood on hand from that day on. We learned later that 54 people in Massachusetts died during the storm, but fortunately my dad made it back home safely. And thank God Ben brought us the wood; we wouldn't have known what to do. Later I thought this was a very considerate thing to do, given that we weren't dating or even talking at that time. And I realized how much I still loved him.

GETTING BIG

My belly was getting bigger. I bought larger pants and baggy shirts, as I still didn't want people to know. I was ashamed and felt kids at school were talking, though they didn't say anything to me. I stopped attending school in April, when I was about five months pregnant; my mom had tutors come to our house for the last two months of the school year. One of them, Mr. B., was the best teacher I'd ever had. I did really well at home with such individual attention, and actually became an A/B student. My morning sickness wasn't so bad any more, and I was thankful for that.

I was about seven months pregnant when it came time for Ben's Senior Prom. He was going to take another girl, which made me sad. I knew he wasn't dating her, but it drove home to me yet again that we really weren't a couple. But then I found out he couldn't go because he'd gotten into trouble at school, and I wasn't sad any more. Around this time I also took my driving test; I'd already had my permit. It was embarrassing, taking the test with my big belly and being so young. I felt the man was looking at me, and was so nervous that I didn't come to a complete stop at a stop sign. But the second time I passed.

The last few months of my pregnancy were a lonely time. Most of my friends no longer called or came over, and I rarely saw Ben. A couple of times he did call without my mom knowing. I told her I was taking my dog Hershey for a walk and met him in the woods. At one point he told me he still cared about me, and I dared to think there was hope for us. But I would still cry in my room, sitting for hours feeling the baby kick inside me, getting more scared the closer the birth got. *What is going to become of me and my baby? Will I be a good mom?* Even when I didn't go to pray on the hill nearby, I was alone and scared and felt He was the only One I could talk to.

Then in June, when I was eight months pregnant, Ben showed up at our house. He told me he loved me and gave me a cheap gold ring. Inside the band it said SARAH. I had no idea what the sex of the baby was, and would only realize later that this was the name of the manufacturer. We kissed and hugged, and he said he wanted to be there for the baby and me. I was so happy, and knew that my mom had been right when she told me to let him go. He did love me. My parents allowed me to see him again, and I began to trust him and think we might spend our lives together.

I had gained 30 pounds in nine months. Wow! I was so big and had stretch marks on my belly. School had ended for the summer, but I still had grades eleven and twelve to go. My mom said she would give up her plans to look for a job, so she could watch the baby and I could finish school. I respected my parents more than ever now; they always worked hard, and now they were making a big sacrifice for me. I was blessed to have a mom and dad who supported me. Not everyone does.

NEW BEGINNINGS

The Fourth of July came and went: no baby. The days dragged by until finally, on July 12, my doctor wanted to see me; there was talk of inducing labor. My mother didn't think that was a good idea. Then Ben's mom, Jan, called and told me to read in the Book of Isaiah, 66:7-14. Verse 9 reads: *"Do I bring to the moment of birth and not give delivery? Says the Lord. Do I close up the womb when I bring to delivery? Says your God."*

We went to the doctor's. I had dilated 3 centimeters and needed to go to the hospital for a further check up. There I was told I was in labor, though I didn't feel I was. But they told me I should stay, and I remember lying on a bed watching *Marcus Welby, M.D.* on TV with my mom. Around 5:00 P.M., the pain started. All they could give me were some shots, but it didn't seem to help. Ben came after he closed up the gas station where he worked; he arrived around 7 P.M., just when the pain was at its worst. They'd just started allowing fathers into the delivery room and the doctor didn't want Ben in there with me, but my mom insisted. Then they gave me a saddle block and I couldn't feel anything from the waist down. The doctor had to use forceps and the baby's shoulders ripped me, but we both made it through the delivery.

"It's a girl!" said the doctor. My daughter was born at 1:02 A.M. on July 13, 1978, and weighed 8 lbs., 1 oz. She was beautiful. They took her away for cleaning up and sewed me up. I was so tired and worn out, I slept all night. The next morning the other new mothers in the room asked me my name. I said Jen, but was still so exhausted they could hardly hear my answer. Then one of the women said, "Don't let anyone take your baby from you!" I promised I wouldn't.

Ben was the one who had thought of the name Sara. Then his mother Jan told us that if you put an "H" at the end of her name it means "the breath of God", because when you sound out the "H" it sounds like a breath. So, our baby daughter Sara would be Sarah Ann.

I carried Sarah, but God gave her breath. She was a beautiful, healthy baby with chubby cheeks. She had black hair and blue eyes, and skin as soft as baby powder. I counted her fingers and toes as every mother does; I was so thankful I had given birth to her. And although it took about a month for the pain of my stitches to feel better, the funny thing is I loved to hear her cry for me. It never upset me or made me mad. She was such a good baby.

Shortly after Sarah's birth, Ben mentioned going into the Air Force. He wanted to go in on the buddy system with his friend Bob, but that wouldn't take place for another year. Meanwhile, Ben got a better paying job with a housecleaning business and in September I went back to school and turned 17. My mom told me I had to grow up and made sure I took responsibility. She watched Sarah during the week, but when I got home from school the baby was mine to care for, along with dirty cloth diapers and homework. My mom also babysat on Saturday nights so Ben and I could go out, but since Sarah had to be asleep first we usually didn't get out until 10 o'clock.

Sarah's first birthday was on Friday the 13th of July, 1979, and Ben and I invited all our friends for a party. It was a beautiful, sunny day and it was hard to believe it had already been a year since her birth. Ben and his friend Bob had signed up for the Air Force and were leaving just before Thanksgiving. I was sad that he was going and knew I would miss him.

That November, I was 18 years old and would graduate in the following May. A week or two before Ben left for Boot Camp, he surprised me by picking me up from school. We drove to the mall and went to a jeweler, where he told me to pick out a ring! I was so excited, I chose a simple, small ring. I think it was a quarter of a karat. I was never a big ring person; I had what I wanted, Ben and my baby girl. Afterwards Ben bought himself a hot dog, and sitting on a bench in the middle of the mall, he said, "Will you marry me?" I answered, "Yes!" and put on the ring. I was so happy to show it to my family, and was sure everything would work out now. God was taking care of me as He'd promised in His Word.

The night before Ben had to leave for Boot Camp, we spent a couple of hours alone. He seemed really scared, and we held each other and talked. The next day Ben, Ricky, Bobby, Sarah and I, and some of our other friends went to the airport to see Ben and Bobby off. It was hard and sad to see him go; I wasn't sure when we'd see each other again. We went to the roof and waved at the plane going down the runway, not knowing if they could see us.

When he was gone Ben and I missed each other and wrote many letters and cards. He wrote me he'd seen us waving from the roof of the airport. The first card read: "Greetings from Lackland AFB Texas. My days belong to my training instructor, but....my nights belong to you." After telling me how busy he was and that he'd been appointed a squad leader, he wrote:

Jen, I want you to know I pray three times a day for you, Sarah and me. I ask him to keep you two safe and close in mind. I miss my beautiful daughter so much because I know that I am missing so much. I hope you send me many pictures so I can watch her grow too. It's hard to write things like this because it makes me start crying, not actually crying but I feel terrible. Anyway it won't be as long as we thought till I see you again, that's the best part of this whole thing. When I see you I won't let you go for 24 hours straight, we will be so happy. I wish I could leave all over again. I would do a lot of things different than I did but it's too late now, so all I can think of is the future.... I miss you and Sarah so much. I just had to drop you a card to say hi. Every drop of love, Ben

On December 20 I wrote Ben a letter from school:

"Ben, I'm in school right now, in study period.... I miss you so much I want you to come home, I miss your kisses and your touch. As I am writing this tears come to my eyes, I love you so much more than I could love any human being. I wish you were here with me so I wouldn't be so depressed and sad. Whenever I think of you words can't say how much I love you because there are no words to describe the love I have for you. Our life together will be so beautiful. There will be laughter, but death too, sadness, but happiness. We will be tried and there will be many hard times.... I will always love you even as our daughter grows and has kids of her own; even when we are grey and old."

I also wrote him in a Valentine's Day card, "I will never regret keeping Sarah. I feel the choice I made was the best. It will probably be the best choice I will ever make in my life ahead, besides marrying the one I love."

Luckily for us, Ben was stationed at Loring Air Force Base in Maine. He had to trade with someone at the last minute, or we would have ended up in Georgia. We were able to see each other at the end of the following February and were married on June 14, 1980. It was a nice wedding, done inexpensively. As I walked down the church aisle with my dad, the "Wedding Song" played with its refrain, *"and there is love ... there is love."*

My dad prepared and served all the food at our wedding. That was a huge effort, and I realized that he'd always shown his love through working so hard to support our family. I'd also wanted to have wine, because of the Bible story when Jesus turned the water into wine at the wedding at Cana; it was our Lord's first miracle. But we hadn't actually planned for it. Then to my delight, Ben's dad Walter showed up at the reception with wine for everyone. He'd also bought us our wedding rings, so both our fathers really showed their support of us. Ben's mom Jan also sang us a special song, playing her guitar. There were about 200 friends and family there, and it was a wonderful day.

The next month was Sarah's second birthday. Wow, two years already! Ben's mother and my mom began to get together and play their guitars. They actually became good friends and would sing Sarah the song, "You Are My Sunshine." Soon Sarah was singing it herself.

Sarah and I joined Ben on the Air Force base just a couple of months later, but it seemed like forever. A neighbor told me about a Sunday babysitting job at a nearby church. One week the workers and children were invited into the Sanctuary during a service. The pastor asked if anyone wanted to invite Jesus into their heart. As he prayed I said the words silently, and felt God's Holy Spirit go through my whole body. Shortly after this, I told Ben about it and learned that he'd responded to a similar invitation at his Baptist church when he was 12. So now we were both Christians, and our time of walking together in the Lord finally began.

I started to go to a Baptist church off-base with Sarah and Ben. There I met a woman named Christine; her husband Phil and my Ben became friends also, although they didn't always attend church on Sundays. She and I were baptized together and attended a Bible study in our neighborhood, where we met other Christian women. Learning about God through studying His Word brought me closer to Him. Though I didn't know it then, it also gave me the strength to meet the challenges that lay ahead for our young marriage.

PROMISES FOR THE FUTURE

Many years have passed, and life has brought many blessings. After Ben had served about eight years in the Air Force, the Lord led him unmistakably out of the military and towards owning his own cleaning business. We have four beautiful daughters: Sarah, Angela, Heather, and Stephanie. I call them my "girlie pearlies", because the smooth white pearls that form from a grain of sand in an oyster shell are so lovely and unique. But while I have loved being a mom, it has not been easy. Ben and I have had a lot of hard times, partly due to our marrying so young; it's only because of God that we are still together. To our dismay, two of our daughters would repeat the mistake I had made, becoming pregnant as teenagers. (Both chose life for their babies.)

But just as He protected me from getting pregnant by the wrong man and from getting an abortion, He has been with us all the way. And I have come to realize that although I love my husband dearly and he is the most important person in my life, only God could take away that empty feeling I had throughout my childhood. So much of my rebellion stemmed from my need for attention, and even protection, that I did not receive from my earthly father. I have long repented of my sins, not only of the premarital sex and nearly getting an abortion, but also for the lies and deceptions I told my parents. It was truly not His plan for me, and I know I saddened Him by what I did, but I am secure in the knowledge that He has forgiven me. Truly He is a compassionate and marvelous Father to those who call on Him.

I was thinking about all of this as the plane prepared to land in Maui. Then we walked through the airport, and there they were. Sarah was holding tiny, newborn Ben; next to her was her husband, T.D. Their three-year-old daughter Nalani Rose stood beside them, holding *lei* for us. I bent down and picked her up, and as I hugged her she put a *lei* on my neck. I kissed her and handed her to her Grampy Ben. Then I reached over to Sarah and little Ben, gave them a hug, and suddenly started weeping. I told Sarah how God had reminded me on the plane about the words He'd given me in 1977, telling me there were sons yet to be born. She looked at me with her big blue teary eyes and said, "I know, I thought the same thing."

I asked God how I should end my story. Then I realized, there is no ending; Sarah has children, and these children will have children. Praise God, this line will continue. Suddenly I had the inspiration which I believe came from God, to tell my story so other babies can be saved.

Part 2

MESSAGES FROM SARAH ANN AND HER FAMILY

Sarah Ann:

A life before birth can seem abstract, detachable, ignorable, and unreal. For a pregnant woman there is only you and your life, a fear of change and of the unknown. At any age, in any circumstance a pregnancy, even planned, can feel daunting, overwhelming and scary. Foreboding emotions are mixed with stress and fear. But life represents possibility, joy, awakening, growth, love, future; life in its purest, natural, most innocent form begins there as we all began, in our mother's womb. To stop a life from birth is to stop an intricate series of events. It is to remove that existence from the many connections, divine and otherwise, that should be allowed to grow. Once conception has occurred, the natural path that life would follow has already been written, possibly for generations to come.

In 1977 a scared teenaged girl chose to give her unborn child the chance to live. That unborn child was me. She did not plan to be a mother at 16. She searched herself, her heart, her faith. She had all the reasons to end my life with abortion, and still she did not. My mother embraced my life, however difficult that was at times, and never looked back. Her choice of life resonates in my very being; her choice of life carries through my very laughter and tears; her choice of life now twinkles in the eyes of my own three children and glows in the arms of my loving husband. Her choice, my life, continues forward towards the future. Her choice, my life, my breath, my heart, and now even the newest life that grew within my womb. That scared 16-year-old girl from 1977 has become a grandmother again. Thank-you so much, Mom, for choosing me.

Life is full of the unknown, but the unknown is not necessarily bad. What can seem overwhelming and impossible one day may become an irreplaceable part of your life the next. Consider that there is a greater plan larger than us and what a blessing it is to be a bringer of life. Consider the voice of the unborn...consider life.

Angela (Sister of Sarah)

I cannot picture my life without my older sister Sarah. She was exactly like an older sister should be: strong, smart, and oh so sweet. I am so grateful to have her; she's someone I always look up to. I also could not picture my life without my two beautiful children. They are loving, happy, smart and beautiful kids. Although I knew premarital sex was wrong, I became pregnant at 17. Many people told me to have an abortion, but I knew that was wrong too. My mother had taught me that very strongly, and at school I'd even given out little plastic models of babies as a pro-life effort to make my friends aware of the reality of a baby's life. I'd urged at least one friend not to abort her pregnancy. I wanted to protect, love and meet my son, and am so glad I did.

I believe that if we abort our children, we rob ourselves, our children, and our future. But most important is that we disappoint God. He could have made humans in any way He wanted, but He chose the female, the mother, to bear life. What a miraculous gift we have as humans, yet through abortion lives are ended with barely a thought for the pricelessness of this gift from the Lord. My children are my life and love, and I'm grateful to the Lord and my mom and dad as well for all their help when I had my children.

Heather Rose (Sister of Sarah)

My parents raised all four of us well. My mother taught us respect, honesty, Christian values, the importance of a relationship with the Lord, and the prevalence of life. I am pro-choice for the baby: I believe every unborn child has a right to choose whether they live or die, and that no baby would choose to die. I also consider myself pro-life, meaning I believe every life is important — even that of the unborn child. My mother also expressed her deep passion for teaching us the facts: that an unborn child, even at conception, is a life, a baby, a living person who immediately starts to grow. She told us that abortion kills that baby, and that the gruesome procedure it takes to end that life is real.

I did great in school; I was the president of my high school Key Club and had many friends. But I also got pregnant at 18, my senior year. My mother had always stressed abstinence, and my parents cried when I told them I was pregnant. They were always there for me, supporting me, but the decision was mine to make. I chose life, and to keep my baby. I believe if my mother had chosen abortion, that might have affected my decision. Now my angel Owen is three; he is the love of my life. I have my own apartment and I am an infant teacher.

Though it wasn't the right decision to have sex before marriage, I made the right decision for my son: I gave him the greatest gift, the gift of life. To help keep me strong through my pregnancy, through parenthood, and through life I remember this verse: "I can do all things through Christ who strengthens me. (Philippians 4:13)

Stephanie Leigh (Sister of Sarah)

If my mother had aborted my sister Sarah, my life would be quite different. I have learned and achieved so much because of her. If it weren't for Sarah, I wouldn't be living in Hawaii, with a great job and a place to live at the age of 20. She has taught me a lot about responsibility and growing up. I have gone to her countless times for advice and comfort, and always come back feeling content. I thank God she is alive, and that I am where I am today. That she escaped the possible abortion that my parents faced all those years ago was no accident; everything happens for a reason. Even if you can't see why until years later, don't give up! Don't abort; one life can change the life of millions.

Ben,   ***husband of Jennifer Mary,***
father of Sarah.

It has been very difficult to me to pen these words of transparency. Three decades after Sarah's birth I still have to drag them out of me reluctantly, fighting tears of shame. But it is so important that other men and women fully understand the devastation of abortion, not only to the baby but to the would-be parents as well. In my case, the guilt of just planning an abortion is still tearing me up. I have asked God, Sarah, Jen, and my family for their forgiveness as I am truly sorry for my wrong decisions. I thank God for changing my mistakes into beautiful blessings as He does so faithfully for His children.

Sarah has always been a blessing to our family. She is beautiful and thoughtful, and while growing up always helped her mom with her three younger sisters. She is a joy to be around, and her happy, can-do spirit lights up a room. She is tenderhearted yet strong; truly inspirational and forgiving; a virtuous woman, lovely and rare. Yet our family of four children and six grandchildren would not exist today if Sarah had not been born.

As a 17-year-old young man back in 1977, I was on the cusp of adulthood with my whole life ahead of me. Summer was coming, my last "vacation" summer as twelfth grade would follow. Though raised in a Christian household, being very immature in some ways filled me with anxiety and feelings of inferiority and selfishness. Being a teenaged boy fueled a strong desire for girls. Fortunately, a family with several cute girls had recently moved into a house near mine. My friend Rick and I introduced ourselves and we all began hanging out. Jennifer and I got along great, and we started dating and getting passionate. She was three months short of 16.

The sexual desires within me, fueled by testosterone, were screaming to be satisfied. I felt that most guys had had sex by now; that I hadn't made me feel less competent or not as good as the majority. After pressure, insistence, and passion, Jen eventually let me have my way. No protection, early release, and a late escape was all it took. What a big mistake this was! Abstinence is a failsafe way to prevent unwanted pregnancy and sexually transmitted diseases; it works 100 percent of the time. I can't stress this enough.

Soon it was obvious Jen was pregnant. *What will we do?* The guilt and shame. *How did this happen? We can't have a baby!* The "just do it" peace-and-love atmosphere of the late seventies had helped spur us on to have sex; now conception, its natural consequence, had followed. Another common part of that culture was, and still is, abortion. *No problem, just kill it.* Of course they couch the act in flowery, politically correct terms, even calling their defenders " Pro Choice". But the real choice is life or death. In those blunt terms, life seems the obvious correct choice.

My choice meant death, though of course I rationalized my decision. *I'm too young. I have my whole life ahead of me, and Jen also. We're still in high school. We can't care for a child. Our parents are going to freak if they find out.* Etc., etc. On the relationship side of things, I did not want to have a family with Jen. I did not see her as my one and only true love. It was more like, "She's cool and I want to get some." End of story.

Not so fast.

Jennifer, a very caring, shy, sensitive girl who lacked confidence, did not want to abort. But I again turned up the pressure, insistence, and domineering manipulation to get her to agree to an abortion. I wanted to kill this new, defenseless, innocent life, this blessing of life. I wanted to squish God's unique and miraculous creation like a bug under my foot so it would never be known. What a selfish, ignorant fool I was! Thank God, He had better plans: the ride I'd arranged to the abortion clinic didn't show up. Shortly thereafter God spoke to Jen, and she decided to have the baby.

What a beautiful baby Sarah was; so precious and lovable! During her first year I grew to love her and Jen so much, I could not imagine them being with anyone else. I wanted to love and care for them both forever. So I freely chose to do that, by marrying Jen and raising Sarah.

No family is perfect, and ours has had its share of troubles and turmoil. But through it all we remember the comforting words of Romans 8:28: "And we know that in all things God works for the good of those who love him, who have been called according to his purpose." (NIV) Praise be to Him!

Jan (Mother of Ben)

When I first met Jenny, I thought she was a sweet girl and was pleased that she was dating my son Ben; little did I know she would become pregnant by him. When that happened, I collapsed. It was the first sorrowful thing to happen to one of my children; Ben was only 17, and Jenny 16. It was much too early for this, and I didn't want my family broken up. I cried and cried, then cried some more. Ben said I was taking it worse than anyone, and I expect he was right.

My husband and I told our son he had to marry Jenny; it was the right thing to do. But that wasn't what sent him over to her house to propose; he did that on his own, in his own way. I am so glad they got married and thankful for their wonderful family. They have been a great blessing to their children and to me and my family as well.

When Sarah was about 3 months old, I was watching her for an afternoon when my ten-year-old daughter, Katy, arrived home from school. She was delighted to see her baby niece at our house. Much to my surprise, because Sarah was asleep, Katy undid the strap on the carry-all, scooped Sarah up in her arms, and carried her down the driveway. She reached the street just in time to hold her up so everyone on the school bus could see her when it returned from down the street. Katy was so proud of her, it took my breath away; I wouldn't have done that, though I loved Sarah dearly. But the Lord showed me that that is how He is with all His children. He loves it when we're lifted up and shown off by those who love us, because there's some of Himself in each person He sends. Whether we're early or late, big or small, talented or limited, He loves us all.

Finally, I think of Jenny as someone who has dared to trust the Lord to work in her life and has seen Him do great things. Here are the words to a song I wrote on trusting Him:

DO WE DARE

Do we dare to trust His love for us, is greater than the
oceans that He made?
Do we dare believe we can receive, this love which all
of our transgressions paid?
Do we dare to feel His love is real, and open up
our hearts to this great love?
Do we dare to face He's made a place, where we
can live and dwell with Him above?

Often we are told that God is love, but in this world
it's often hard to see,
It's hard to think He could possibly love us,
that if we trust His love will set us free.
But He's someone who'll never let us down,
He'll love us more than parent, brother, friend,
And if we come to trust that it is so, we will walk in
love that never ends.

Do we dare to hope He'll help us cope, that He'll
be there when all else is gone?
Do we dare to bring love to our King, and sing to
Him our very sweetest song?
Do we dare to say Love's found a way, to dwell
in our heart and make us whole?
Do we dare to live, our lives to give, and share
the hope and love that's in our soul?

Jenny and Ben dared to do what this song says, and He made
a way for them. I pray that if you become pregnant, you will have
your baby and come to know your precious child. You'll be glad you
did. God bless you.

Part 3

THE PAIN ABORTION CAUSES

H ere are the real stories, in their own words, of women and men who have been hurt by abortion, including one whose adult daughter lost her life. I pray that those who are still not fully healed will be blessed by their willingness to share their stories.

Christine

When I think back to my state of mind at age 15, I wonder how I made any of the decisions I made. But the one that most interwove terrible guilt and shame into the years that followed was my decision to have an abortion.

I've heard so many views and opinions about abortion, from the selfishness some believe the decision comes from, to the despair others have experienced. For me, the single word I would use in regards to my abortion was "guilt". Oh, the heaviness of that word! The pangs of it would come, sometimes out of nowhere, or from an article in a magazine or a story on the television. Wherever it came from, the same jolt of "You are guilty of taking someone's life" would ring through my head. There was nowhere to hide from it. I was living life "on the outside" but felt, from the depths of my soul, that I was emotionally imprisoned.

As I looked around the room at the other young girls in the clinic that day, I'd wondered if they felt the same way. I was at least lucky to have the support of my boyfriend, who is now my husband for over 25 years, and my mother. But I can still picture the girls who sat there all alone that day, and years later would think of them from time to time, pondering whether they'd suffered for so many years as I did.

I believe that I suffered with guilt for over two decades because I was brought up believing that if I did something wrong or bad, God was not just mad at me, but hated me and cursed me, so to speak, with a life of never-ending guilt. I was weighted down by a big sign saying "Murderer!" that I carried on my back everywhere I went.

Today, after being blessed with two very sweet boys (actually young men, ages 25 and 22), I can honestly tell you that I don't carry that heavy load and label anymore. There is one reason only why I don't. It's not because it never happened, or that I pretend it didn't, and it's not because I came to believe it was acceptable to have had an abortion. It was because one night, while praying and being prayed over, I gave my guilt to God. The same God, who I once feared, suddenly needed me, and I wanted to know Him.

I have gone through both physical and mental handicaps in my life, and God used those terrible experiences for His glory by bringing me to my knees begging for forgiveness. Because He gave His Son and let Him die for my sins (including my abortion), and then because His Son gave me the gift of His Spirit as He went to sit at the right hand of His Father, I can now stand tall without the weight of the guilt. That was something only God could do. I not only received forgiveness from the grace of God, but also love I never knew was possible.

I will not say a pang doesn't come when I hear the word "abortion" or read something about it. But it is a pang of grief, not guilt and shame, and I give it to God. I also know He has been watching over the child I gave to him on April 20, 1979, 31 years ago.

Christine named her baby Angel.

Rick

I met my girl friend when she was 21. She lived with her mother, but eventually we got a place of our own. She became pregnant and we discussed whether to have the baby. I told her she should, that we

48

could work it out. But she said she couldn't have a baby just then, because we were not ready and she would lose her job.

I did not believe in abortion. I knew it was wrong, but she was going to do it anyway. I dropped her at a clinic in Boston; she didn't want me to go in with her. When I came back to get her, she looked pretty shook up. It was bad. But she got pregnant three more times and decided to get an abortion each time, even though I urged her every time to keep it. She was so vein, only thought of herself and her looks, she made me feel I wasn't good enough for her.

Shortly after the last abortion, my girlfriend left me for another man. I have always felt awful about it, and am ashamed that we used abortion as birth control.

Now I am 49, and I feel I'm to old to have children.

April

When I was 15, I met my first boyfriend. We lived in different states at the time: he was in New York, I in Massachusetts. Within three days of knowing me, he made a move on me and I said no. He stopped, so I thought he respected me. We would talk every day and everything was sort of rushed on an emotional level. He was my first real boyfriend, and I allowed myself to fall harder than I was ready for.

When he came back to Massachusetts, everything was rushed on a more sexual level. He stole my virginity from me. I placed myself in a situation where a man was abusing me emotionally, sexually, and physically. I even allowed him to live in my house with me when his mother kicked him out. At this point I had lost all levels of self-esteem. My world seemed to be crashing down in front of me.

Things became worse. He was controlling me and having people watch my every move. He would physically hurt me and even threatened to kill me. But I didn't know how to get out of the situation and thought, *This is what I deserve; this is how it is supposed to be.* I'd never had much confidence, and he destroyed the little I had left.

Eventually my friends got sick of his abusive treatment of me and pressed charges. I ended up saving him and getting him out of jail. The court placed a restraining order on him; we didn't follow it and snuck around to meet each other. Our parents even helped us to see each other! I couldn't stay away from him; I was also afraid he'd come after me.

~~

Whenever we would have sex I would just lie there and take it. I felt pain and suffering. He would always pull out on time, but one day he didn't. I know now, though I did not then, that he did it on purpose. My instincts said, *This is it; I'm going to be pregnant.* Of course I had to wait to find out, and I felt scared and nervous. I'd had a pregnancy scare before this, and that boyfriend had been hurt I wasn't pregnant! This time, after I missed my period, I told my mom I needed a pregnancy test. Sure enough, it was positive. Even though I'd felt I was pregnant, it was nothing like actually knowing. I broke down, crying hysterically. My mom tried to hug me, but I just didn't want to be touched. I was confused and hurt. It's not that I didn't want children, but I was only 16. I felt I was in a nightmare. *How could this happen to me?*

My mom told my boyfriend's mother, because she couldn't handle it alone. They had me take another test. I took *three* tests, all positive. When my pregnancy began, abortion wasn't even a thought in my mind; I'd always been against it. I was sure I wanted to have and keep the baby, but things consistently got worse. My boyfriend and even his family kept asking me to have an abortion; my mother wanted me to keep the baby. I was in a constant fight with myself and all of them.

During the two months I was pregnant, I was crying constantly. I had morning sickness the whole second month. But I remember touching my stomach, thinking *There's a baby in there.* I had an instinct it would be a girl. I thought, *Maybe I can do an adoption —* but my boyfriend and his family threatened to take my child away if I did. I would never allow any of them to raise my child. Finally I realized I was in an abusive relationship and wasn't financially stable enough to do this. So I decided to get an abortion. It was so hard, and I still feel like I was forced into it. But I don't think I could have had a child with him. What if he hurt the baby? I didn't want that to happen. The days before the procedure, I prayed for a miscarriage. I didn't want to go through with it.

~~

The first time I tried to go for the abortion, I went to a hospital in Boston with my mom, my then ex-boyfriend, and his mom. I was vomiting in the parking lot, and when I went in I freaked out and wouldn't get the needle that would sedate me. They said, "Maybe you don't want to do this." I knew I didn't, but I didn't feel I had any other choice. I left, and my ex and his mom weren't happy. So I made a second appointment. And it was the same thing: the whole morning I was vomiting. This time I actually went through with the needle and tried to do the procedure. I remember the doctor touching me; it was painful and uncomfortable. He got angry with me and said, "I can't work under these conditions." This time I was with my mom, my ex-boyfriend, and his grandmother. There was just so much pressure, but I honestly didn't want to do it. The doctor realized this, and refused to carry through with the abortion.

The third time I went to a clinic, there were pro-life people outside. As before, I was throwing up all morning. Then I remember sitting in the room, asking if they'd put the medicine in the IV yet. That was it; it was the end of it. I awoke still drugged and with cramps. They asked if I was okay, and I went to the bathroom and then left. I felt confused and drugged up as I walked out with my ex-boyfriend.

~~

I couldn't talk about getting an abortion. I just pretended it didn't happen, since I couldn't face the reality of it. But a year later I was watching a "Lifetime" movie, and one simple line was stated: "I'll never get to see pictures of my baby." I fell apart, crying for what seemed like forever. I blamed myself and felt like a horrible person. I felt I didn't deserve to exist, and hated myself for what I had done. I realized I hadn't been able to think about it because I could never forgive myself.

I was only able to cry one other time. This year I forced myself to look at abortion pictures to show myself what I did. I know this wasn't the best method, but I still feel horrible. Why can't I deal with it? I don't know how to deal with it full-on. It's like it never happened, yet it did. When I see people my age with babies, it makes me want one so badly.

Over the summer my "ex" had a baby with another girl, and I could not believe it. I thought, *Why does he get to have a child?* I am still so angry and hurt. I am afraid I will be punished and never have children. I just want to be able to face this and forgive myself.

April's abortion was 10 years ago. She named her baby Angelina Nicole.

Rich

My girlfriend was 18 years old when I met her. She grew up as an Irish Catholic, in a family of 12 children. I got her pregnant. Even though society said it was okay to have an abortion, deep down I knew it was wrong. But I had fallen away from God at this time, and so I turned against her. I called her bad names and told her to stay away from me. She would talk about names for the baby, and her parents wanted her to have it and keep it. But my plan was to separate from her.

Knowing she really wanted to be with me, I told her I would stay with her if she had the abortion. So she went against her parents' wishes and her own, because she loved me and thought I would stay with her. I actually did stay a couple of months, but I couldn't stay with her longer because of my guilt and pain over the abortion. She was a constant reminder of what I'd caused her to do.

I buried the pain deep inside me; I didn't think of it for 20 years. But then I got sober and began to do the right things. I married and had a baby girl. I started attending a 12-Step group and realized I needed to make amends with my old girlfriend. One day when I was in a grocery store, I saw her. I was afraid, because I thought she would hate me for what I'd made her do. But I had to "go for it" and tell her how sorry I was. So I approached her. She said she was well—she'd married and had two children — and asked me how I was. I told her I wasn't doing too well and that I needed to talk with her. She agreed.

No one came down the aisle at the store the whole time we were talking. I told her how badly I felt for the way I'd treated her, and that I'd made her have the abortion. She forgave me, and we both cried. Right then I felt an evil spirit lift off me. Jesus healed me and I felt free.

I asked God for forgiveness for the baby I threw away. Then I had to forgive myself. I am sorry for what I did, but I know He's forgiven me. I am now a strong Christian in the Lord; Jesus went to the cross for my sins. Many men stuff the pain down, but if you get healed you will feel the freedom that Jesus died to give you.

Stephanie

My name is Stephanie, and I am 60 years old. At 26, when I decided to have an abortion, I was a selfish and self-centered woman who was afraid of being alone and taking care of myself. I wanted someone to take care of me. It was not until I was 27 years old and started 12-Step Recovery that I finally went to the only One who could really fill that empty hole I had in my heart and soul: God. He is now who I want to please. Here is my story.

I grew up in a middle-class family with strict and religious moral beliefs. My mother was a dedicated church member, who loved and feared the Lord. She lived her beliefs. My dad had grown up attending church. He chose not to be a church member, but lived a moral life-style. I grew up loving God and wanting to please Him by being a "good girl". I became very involved in my church, and felt accepted and nurtured there. I did not feel this at home with my family. That being said, I also grew up very insecure. I believed that I was not as good as my older sister, and that my parents loved her more than me. I became a very fearful and unhappy child. At age four, I just couldn't stand my feelings of fear, doubt of my parents' love, and that I had any value. Then I found that by eating large quantities of "junk" food and being a "people pleaser", I could escape those uncomfortable and scary feelings. Then when I turned 12, I became physically developed and received a lot of attention from boys in my class. Wow, this was even better at giving me a feeling of accep-

tance, importance, and freedom from the fear of not being worth
anything. So, I became an attention addict, craving attention from
men. I was looking for "love" in all the wrong places.

At 25, I became an alcoholic. I couldn't stop drinking even
though it was interfering with me working and doing a decent job. It
was causing me to lose the few friends I had. I was acting out sexually in ways I had never done before, roaming the bars for one-night
stands just to get a little attention and feel cared about. Even if the
price was having sex, when all I wanted was someone to talk to.

The following year, I was a full-time college student. My pro-
miscuous lifestyle was getting old; I was known around the bars and
not so popular any more. On New Year's Eve there was a bigger
than usual crowd at one of my "bars", and I caught the eye of a "new
man". I started a conversation, and he stayed and talked with me; I
was so happy and exhilarated. When the last call was announced,
we had one more drink and went to his apartment. That night I con-
ceived my baby. This man was a gambler and I gave him money
and my T.V. just to keep him around, but when his steady girlfriend
came out from the background after a month or two we parted ways.

Around March I started to feel sick to my stomach and very
tired. It was harder and harder to get up for my classes, and I craved
ice cream and sleep. All of a sudden it dawned on me that I had
not had my menstrual time for a few months. It hit me like a ton of
bricks, *I'm pregnant!* I denied it for a few weeks, but I kept getting
sick every morning and still no menstrual time. So I went to the Bill
Beard clinic in Boston, where my pregnancy test came back positive. I cried, and they advised me on getting an abortion. I went back
to my apartment in a daze, and made a trip out to my parents' house.
I lied to my mother about needing $200, telling her a friend needed
an abortion. She was holding my own money for me, so could not
refuse.

The next day, I went to the abortion clinic. After another pregnancy test they took me right into a room and performed the abortion. No one counseled me that I could keep the baby and give it up
for adoption; no one talked to me about what would happen during
the procedure. I was just escorted to the abortion room, told to put
on a gown, and given a shot to put me out. In the recovery room,

I finally woke up to how serious a mistake I had made. I had murdered a baby, and God was not going to be very happy with me. I cried for myself, not the baby; I was scared. Even then, no one came to talk to me or to give me any counsel. They just handed me my clothes and led me out the door. Totally numb, I went out and got drunk that night and slept with some man I didn't know very well. They had told me not to have intercourse for a few weeks! But I had to numb my feelings of extreme guilt and fear of God.

A year later, I finally found the halls of 12-Step Recovery. I entered Alcoholics Anonymous and got sober; four months later, I found joined Overeaters Anonymous. When I took away the "drugs" that were keeping my feelings stuffed down, I became even more shameful, guilty, and remorseful about having aborted my baby. These feelings kept me in a deep depression and kept me going back to junk food to numb the feelings as I had when I was a young child. The feelings of not wanting to live anymore were getting stronger and stronger. I worked for a psychiatrist at the time, and finally I told him my story and how deep my depression was. He put me on an antidepressant, which helped a little.

During this time though, God came into my life through working the Twelve Steps in both AA and OA. I went back to church, and tried to get right with God. I went to an OA retreat at this time, and was offered a one-on-one confession time with a priest. I made a confession about the abortion. He asked me where I thought the baby was, and I said with Jesus in heaven. He asked if I wanted to "talk" to the baby, which I did. I acknowledged my baby for the first time and asked her forgiveness for aborting her. I then asked God to forgive me, cried a lot, and was truly repentant. I left there feeling free from the bondage of my sinful behavior and allowed thoughts of the baby, the abortion, and my feelings of deep regret to settle deep into my heart and psyche.

Zip forward 32 years. I had seldom thought about the baby or the abortion and had never talked about it to anyone except my now-husband. I'd just tried to ignore the issue and my own experience. Then one Sunday, a friend from church told me she was taking a Bible study through an organization called A Women's Concern, to uncover her feelings about having had an abortion. I thought, *I've dealt with that issue, good for her,* and thought nothing more about it.

Then last October I was sitting alone in a room at a women's conference, reading the Bible and praying, because I'd offered to be available if anyone wanted to talk or pray with someone. Along came my friend, who'd just attended a banquet for women who'd gone through the post-abortion Bible study. She'd asked anyone in the audience to come up and give her a hug if they, too, had had an abortion. As she explained that it was the first time she'd publicly admitted to having an abortion, I spontaneously gave her a hug. She looked at me with confusion, then "got" it. She said, "I bet you have wanted to tell me this for a long time." I told her, "No, I haven't, but I do now." I then told her the story of my abortion. I cried and cried, and was confused as to why I was so emotionally moved. Then I realized that while I had felt forgiven, nothing had been resolved for me about the enormity of what I had done: what I'd lost in not having the baby, and how I'd tried to keep it all tucked away from myself.

The post-abortive Bible study was an hour away and not a convenient time of year, but I went anyway; I knew this was "my time" to finally deal with having had an abortion at 26. This extensive eight-week course, which used the book *Forgiven and Set Free* by Linda Cochrane taught me about the nature of God, His willingness to forgive me for the abortion if I asked Him, and all the other feelings — denial, anger, depression, loss –that I had buried deep inside myself. The intimate group setting helped me process emotionally what I was uncovering; everyone was so supportive, accepting wherever I was that day on my journey out of self-protective denial. I was encouraged to journal my thoughts and feelings. I slowly realized that I'd never once thought of the baby; I'd only cared about how I would look to other people if I announced I was pregnant and unmarried.

I also recognized that I'd never mourned the many losses that follow choosing abortion instead of life. The caring and nurturing environment of the group members and the loving, forgiving God I met in the Bible gave me a safe place to start the grieving process for the baby I could have had, but chose not to. I came to accept that not only had the baby lost her life, I too had lost a great deal: I'd lost the mother/child relationship with my daughter that I so cherished having with my son.

When I let down my defenses and let myself be "real" with my emotions, the grief was huge. I allowed my husband to be in on my process, as well as my group. I also drew very close to my Lord and Savior, Jesus, who was my refuge when I thought I couldn't get through the sadness and regret. I never tried to run away from the feelings, yet did put some healthy boundaries around them. I felt my feelings, did my grieving, and talked to appropriate people.

Towards the end of the Bible study, I was asked to give my baby a name and a memorial service. I had always known that my baby was a girl, and I named her Sarah Martha. I wrote her a letter, saying everything in my heart I needed to say, and gave her the type of memorial service I would give to anyone I love and cherish. I found poems and lullabies that said exactly what I felt about her, and played them for her. I had an embroidery announcement made, and put a lovely basket of pink dried flowers on the table. The Bible study, the group sharing, my quiet time with God, and the grief work all helped in the grieving process, but giving her the memorial service gave me the closure I needed until I meet her in heaven.

This process of acknowledging my decision to abort my baby and the ramifications to the baby, myself, my family, and society at large has been so healing for me personally. Now, it's time for me to help other women. I have committed myself to speaking out against abortion by telling others my story and how very deeply my abortion affected me. Today I would do everything so differently. I can't go back, but I can help another women avoid the regret and remorse that I will live with for the rest of my life because I chose to abort rather than give my baby life.

Jimmy

In 1983 my girlfriend and I were very close. We had dated for awhile when she became pregnant, so a decision had to be made about the baby. We agreed on an abortion because she had just started college and wanted to have a career. She said that was more important than having a baby right then. I had my own feelings about it, but I just gave in to what she wanted.

I told her I would be with her through the abortion, and we went to a "family planning" center. The place had a very strange feeling to it, and of course we were thinking about what we were doing. We were young, and it weighed on us a great deal; it felt like a doctor's appointment with an edge. We didn't know anyone there, so there was no personal connection.

We went in, and they showed us to our room. Someone came and talked to us for five minutes. They put my girlfriend on the table, and I held her hand. There were tools. I couldn't believe it was going to take place right there. They put some kind of a pan under her, and whatever came out went into this pan and flushed down a hole and then fell into a sink. The doctor rinsed out the pan. That's when it really hit me hard. That was my baby.

I hate to say it, but we took a life. My girlfriend was upset, but I felt I was more disturbed than she was. The visit was so fast! We were in and out of there more quickly than getting a tooth pulled. She went on to have three more abortions with other men, but sadly has had no children.

I got married and have been blessed with two daughters.

Laurie

As an angry and rebellious young woman, I found myself using promiscuity to have control over my own body and life. No one could stop me. It was a double edged sword of making me feel better in some ways, only to have the pendulum blade swing back with shame as my reputation in a small town was ruined. My first pregnancy terrified me: I thought of how much worse my social situation would get and was desperate not to be pregnant any more. Self-hatred and aggression toward what was growing inside me had me punching my belly; there was no way I was going to have that baby.

No one outside my immediate family and the young man and his family had any idea of what I was going through. I was not allowed to talk about the abortion, and no one ever mentioned it to me afterwards. The experience was horrendous. I was awake and in agony throughout the procedure. I'd never had menstrual cramps before, though I was almost seventeen, and they told me to stop crying because I was scaring the other girls who were waiting for their turn on the table. The horror of that first abortion was never dealt with. There was no one to talk to about it and the self-recrimination left me feeling that I deserved whatever misery I suffered for what I had done to my baby. My mother and grandmother had taken me, and I remember how surreal it was for us to stop for lunch on the way home as if nothing had happened and my very being wasn't in crisis.

As soon as it was over, I knew I had done a terrible thing. My father, who I was with only for scheduled weekends and vacations since his divorce from my mother when I was four, took me to an obstetrician friend of his for my follow-up visit and made sure I had some form of birth control. I continued my Junior year of high school before moving away from my mother to go back to my old town to live with a friend where I had grown up. I continued being sexually active because it was the only love I felt in my life; since it wasn't adultery, I justified it as being ok. (I didn't know the definition of fornication at the time or that biblical standards do actually apply to these actions.)

The deeper assault came when I gave in to having the second abortion, while fully knowing what it would cost me and that it was wrong. My fear of losing this man who would become my husband was rooted in a powerfully dysfunctional co-dependence that I didn't yet know I had. It was a pressure I had no defense against. The best self-protection I could manage for myself was to insist on going to a place where they would put me to sleep so I would not have to hear, see, and smell the terror of the experience again. As years went by and I helped my husband raise my step-children and had a son of our own, I developed depression and was diagnosed with PostTraumatic Stress Disorder. I had suicidal ideation and caught myself almost striking my precious son before realizing I needed more help than anti-depressants and counseling could provide. I had to begin being brutally honest with myself about myself as I leaned into God to help me heal my greatly damaged psyche.

It is germane to my story to relate that I had accepted Christ as a child; the rebellion of my adolescence had been about anger with God over my family dysfunction and the emotional and sexual abuse from my childhood that was never addressed or acknowledged. I'd found my acceptance and love in sex, people-pleasing, and over-achieving rather than in the security of a family that nurtured and cared about my woundedness. Being raised in the church gave no answer to this problem in my life.

As an adult, though, I grew in understanding of the Lord and knew He had forgiven me for the things I had done. This included the abortions I'd had, yet there was still no healing of the trauma or loss. I could not look at or think about the things that were still wounding me because there was no one to talk to about it. It was too painful, and I still had no one to blame but myself. I attended church and had a growing walk with God that strengthened my life. But abortion was always held up as the worst thing anyone could do, and so criticized that I would never have admitted I was one of those horrible women who killed not one, but two of her own children in flagrant disregard for the sanctity of their lives. That my own life and well-being had been forfeited in the process would not, in my mind, have quelled the wagging tongues of my God-fearing, wonderful, pro-life brothers and sisters who worshipped with me every Sunday.

So I learned not to think about the abortions and pressed on with my life. I did the best I could to love and raise my son, but I always 'knew' I was a terrible mother. God and my mother eventually brought me to a ministry where I was loved and allowed to grow and serve Him, and it was there that I was invited to attend an abortion healing retreat weekend. I am so grateful for the women who came and shared their stories, and who had developed a course of biblical study that pierced the hidden darkness in my soul. All the pain and silence still kept me from mourning the loss of my babies. Their firsthand understanding and compassion gave me the support I needed to face the full magnitude of the monster that day by day ate away at my peace, much like hidden carpenter ants slowly devour the structural integrity of a building's walls without the owner's awareness. I cry as I write this, knowing that April and Logan now have names and I am assured they are in Heaven rooting me on in my life to be the woman God created me to be, but who the enemy nearly destroyed through the demonic weapon of a "woman's right to choose."

I wish I could say that Christianity's pro-life movement was helpful to me in my healing, but their current stance and approach to stopping abortion does not address the bigger atrocity of what this does to women. I believe that women must be educated about the effects of abortion on our ability to bond with other children, as well as on our own self-image with regards to our natural purpose and instinct as nurturers and mothers.

Today I choose life and love in Christ and I know that without a doubt, no matter how low a person falls from grace, through poor choices of any kind, *His* grace is sufficient. It is He who heals and restores the broken wastelands of the human soul. Through the power of His love in His Word and in His servants who are willing to share in His restorative work, there is hope for joy and peace to come to devastated souls in despair. Thank you, Lord, for saving mine.

As part of the memorial service for our babies the ladies and myself at the recovery weekend were asked to prepare something to share to honor our children that we lost to abortion. A poem for April and song for Logan were gifts from the Lord. With love and hope that my sharing may reach another hurting sister or brother who has yet to grieve for the loss of their child, I remain, Laurie: loving mother, survivor and over comer in Christ.

Laura

Laura Hope Smith lived in extreme poverty in Honduras until she was adopted at the age of five by Eileen and Tom Smith of Sandwich, Massachusetts. By all accounts Laura was sweet and pleasant, vibrant, loving, and caring. As she grew, she had a good word for everyone she met and encouraged others with her optimistic views. Then she became engaged to a soldier who serves in Iraq and became pregnant.

No one ever thought Laura would die having an abortion. But in her last conversation with her mother, Laura asked for extra spending money; her mother had no idea she was pregnant or how she planned on using it. On September 13, 2007, 22-year-old Laura

Hope Smith died from complications that arose during her abortion in Hyannis.

The family had just started watching television after dinner that evening when the telephone rang. Laura's name was on the caller I.D. They always loved to hear from her, because she lifted their spirits. But instead of Laura on the phone it was her girlfriend Karen, crying loudly; Laura had had an abortion, wasn't breathing, and had been shipped to the hospital. She'd actually died at the abortion clinic, but the hospital could only tell that to a family member. So the doctor came on the phone and told her mother the news.

Life stopped for Laura's parents and three siblings; they were shocked and devastated. Searching for answers, Eileen met with the doctor who performed Laura's abortion at his former office in Hyannis. When asked if he believed Laura's death to be his fault, he said, "I wracked my brain to think of what I could have done differently." He claimed that Laura would have died regardless of how he had performed the abortion. But Eileen has read the medical reports and believes that Laura's death was his fault. She was shocked by the details she unearthed about his practice: "He has no medical staff, just a receptionist and a hand holder," she said. "This doctor is practicing third-world medicine in the medical Mecca of the world. This goes beyond medical negligence."

Eileen went to the Lord in grief and prayed He would bring something good out of Laura's death so she could bear the pain. God answered that prayer: "I believe God has opened my eyes," Eileen says. "I have always been pro-life, but I kept it in my heart. I thought the abortion protesters were spitting in the wind and abortion was here to stay. It took the death of my daughter for me to become active in the fight against it." Although Eileen will never know why Laura, who was staunchly pro-life, chose to have an abortion, she believes part of her decision may have stemmed from ignorance about what actually happens during the procedure. "I don't believe she knew what she was doing," Eileen said. "Children today are taught to think that abortion is just removing a blob of tissue. I as a parent didn't do enough."

The church must educate its members about abortion, Eileen maintains. But it must also show love and compassion to unwed mothers and women who have abortions, rather than stigmatize them. In the last ten years there has been a new awareness within the pro-life moment that it is important to treat the mother as a victim also.

Eileen's message of abortion education extends beyond the church. She believes abortions will continue until every person in the world knows that "a baby is ripped limb from limb." In England, the British TV program *Dispatches* showed an abortion procedure and numerous images of aborted infants, resulting in indignation from the media and abortion rights supporters.

Here in the U.S., Eileen experienced the media's reluctance to discuss the harmful nature of an abortion. The local media largely ignored Laura's tragedy and the *Cape Cod Times* only reported it weeks after it occurred. But in September 2010, on the third anniversary of Laura's death, her abortionist pled guilty to manslaughter. The next day he was sentenced to three months in jail. Eileen hopes that this will make other abortionists take notice.

Today, Eileen's desire is to bring her message to pastors, parents, educators, pregnancy care centers, and adolescents. "I know that God is going to bring good out of my daughter's death; we're going very public with a very shameful, private thing because I believe God wants to use it to save lives." She has spoken about Laura's story all over the country with amazing results. She says she feels empowered, emboldened, and emblazoned by the Holy Spirit to speak, not to the secular world, but to the church with a message. "Every time I speak, I believe I put another nail in the coffin of the abortion industry. Abortion can end in our lifetime," she believes, and tells her listeners how. Laura's story moves them deeply as they hear about "the beauty from ashes", told from a mother's heart.

(Operation Rescue named Eileen Smith their Person of the year for 2010. She can be contacted to speak to groups and gatherings through their web site, www.VoicesOfTruth.net. Information was taken from The Cape Cod Times, with permission from Eileen Smith)

Part 4

CHOOSE LIFE

I hope and pray that if you are pregnant, these stories will help you to choose Life. That should be the only choice; no one should have the right to end that new life in your womb. I'm not perfect. I sinned by having premarital sex and almost made a terrible choice in an effort to correct that, but I have long realized I didn't have that "right". My daughter Sarah was already being created in my womb, where a baby is supposed to be safe and warm. Your child, too, should be given the chance to grow

Here are some verses of Scripture that show God's heart for the human beings He created:

"The spirit of God hath made me, and the breath of the almighty hath given me life. And the Lord God formed man of the dust of the ground and breathed into his nostrils the breath of life, and man became a living soul." Genesis 2:7

"I praise you because I am fearfully and wonderfully made; your works are wonderful, I know that full well. My frame was not hidden from you when I was made in that secret place. When I was woven together in the depths of the earth, your eyes saw my unformed body. All the days ordained for me were written in your book before one of them came to be." Psalm *139: 14-16*

"Children are a heritage of the Lord: and the fruit of the womb is his reward." Psalm *127:3*

If you are not pregnant, the best thing you could do is save yourself for the man you will marry. People say to me, "You can't tell kids that!" I tell them, "We are not animals. We're made in the image of God and know right from wrong. If God tells us to wait, then with His help we can. It's the world that tells us we can't and that we shouldn't have to. We're even told that and handed condoms in our health classes at school. But there are also a lot of sexual diseases out there that can kill you and some that can hurt your baby, even killing them, so please save yourself for marriage. When you say you are for Life, then only be for Life. There is no middle ground here, only Life or Death. That's the choice. It's hard to hear, but it's true.

People say, "What if I was raped?" When I hear that, it sounds so painful. Although what happened to me is called date rape today, I have no idea how I would feel if I were raped by a stranger. But the baby in your womb is innocent, and part of you too. That baby's right to live should not be taken away because the man who did this act was bad. Please think about carrying the baby to term, whether or not you choose to parent afterwards.

People say to me, "What about the people in Third World countries who have too many illegitimate children?" I say, "The wisdom of the Scriptures are for everyone, regardless of where they live. These are intelligent people, aren't they? Those babies have a right to be born as much as any others."

Another argument I hear is, "It's my body!" That's true, but once you are pregnant you have a God-given responsibility over the new life within you as well. A growing baby is a whole new person. Some people say, "What if my baby is going to be disabled?" If that's the case, then I'm sad for you and for your baby. But he or she is still a person created by God, with the right to live and be loved.

Girls also say, "It will be too hard to give my baby away!" I have heard that there are as many people wanting to adopt a child as there are abortions each year. I know it would be terribly difficult to place a child you have carried, but wouldn't it be better for both of you than having an abortion? So, please — give birth, and if you can't keep the baby, give him or her to a couple who are praying for a child. Take responsibility for your actions, and pray for the faith to believe that the Lord will aid all who trust in Him.

Choose *Life!*

A CHANCE TO HEAL

We have a good and loving God, who knows you more than you know yourself. If you have had an abortion and come to believe it was a mistake, there is forgiveness through Him. If you want to experience this forgiveness and learn how to draw closer to this amazing God, please read what He says in the Scriptures:

"If we say that we have no sin, we deceive ourselves, and the truth is not in us. If we confess our sins, he is faithful and just to forgive us our sins, and to cleanse us from all unrighteousness." 1 John 1:8, 9

Tell the Lord what you have done, then ask Him to forgive you for all your sins and ask the Lord to come live in you. Then you will live for Him as well, and be blessed more than you can imagine. My own life is proof of His grace.

" And Jesus said unto her, neither do I condemn thee: go, and sin no more." John 8:11

On Ben's and my 30th wedding anniversary, I was writing in my journal when the Lord led me to write a prayer that I began to pray every day. I am glad to share it with you, that you may make it yours as well if you wish:

Make Me More Like You

"Lord, make me more like you; fill me with the Holy Spirit!
Let your thoughts be my thoughts, let my eyes see what yours see,
let my ears hear what yours hear, let my lips speak what you would
speak. Let my hands do, touch, and heal what your hands would
do, let my feet walk where you would walk. I give my whole self
to you; use me, Lord for your glory not mine; teach me to be a
servant like you. I don't want any part of what this world has to
offer, I just want to live for you; then one day when my time comes
to be with you, I would love to hear, "Well done,
my good and faithful servant!"
There will be no more pain, no more tears, no more sadness.
Thank you Lord for choosing me, because I am
not worthy. In JESUS' Name, Amen.

Finally, if you are pregnant and would like to talk to someone or if you are struggling because you have had an abortion, the National Right to Life Committee has information at www.NRLC.org.. There are also state pro-life organizations whose websites are easily available; they should be able to tell you about crisis pregnancy center near you. If you live in Massachusetts, check out the website www.FRIENDSOFAWOMANSCONCERN.ORG.

WHO GIVES BREATH?
NAME YOUR BABY!

If you would like to give the baby you or your partner aborted a name (or have already done so), please contact me at **www. thebreathofgod.vpweb.com**. I am planning to use some of the proceeds from this book to make a memorial where these babies' names will be engraved on a stone. This will be one or more actual places where mothers and fathers can go and see their baby's name, helping them to find closure and forgiveness by God. My dream is to have a day when we can all come together in the memory of these precious babies and celebrate our healing.

This memorial will help others see that abortion not only kills a baby, it hurts the mother (and father) too. I hope it will encourage others to choose life instead of making this terrible mistake. So please, speak out for your baby and other babies that could be aborted. People also need to know that girls die having abortions; if anyone has lost a daughter, sister, or other relative or friend because she had an abortion, please put her first name, then the name of the baby.

One day God told me something to tell those who have had an abortion. I still hear it every day in my head; in my mind I can see women weeping, and I become very emotional. He said to tell you: "I hear your prayers, I see your tears, and I feel your pain. Come to Me!" After writing this, I wanted to be sure and asked the Lord, "Is this what you want me to tell the women?" Then I went to bed, and the next morning the name Hezekiah kept coming to me. I immediately wrote it down on a piece of paper so I wouldn't forget. Then I made a cup of coffee and sat down with my Bible. I looked up "Hezekiah" and read about the Lord telling Isaiah to tell Hezekiah, the leader of His people: *I have heard your prayer and seen your tears; I will heal you." (2 Kings 20:4-5)*

I was amazed. God answered me and let me know through His Word that when we pray and cry out to Him, He *wants* to heal us. The Lord also impressed on me that He has put within each of our hearts something for us to do; you know who you are. Make sure it is from the Lord, then do it.

Let's stop abortion: give your baby a name! Thank you.

Jennifer Mary

Also if you would like to know Gods Miraculous Encouragement: The story Behind This Book, go to my web site.
www.thebreathofgod.vpweb.com

ACKNOWLEDGMENTS

I owe a debt to my loving, and patient mother in law Janice and to her good friend Lori, who helped put this book together. Also to my mom who helped get the book published, and to a Father and Mom of a special church who are such a blessing. Also to the men and women who shared their stories of pain that abortion causes, thank you. I could not have done this without you. Baby's lives will be saved.

My love to my Girlie Pearlies"for the encouragement they gave me.

I appreciate my beautiful family, I am so blessed.

To my husband Ben of 31 years, thank you for believing in me that with Gods help I could do this. You are my best friend. GOD BLESS YOU ALL!

TO MY LORD, MY GOD, MY SAVIOR JESUS CHRIST!

I give all the praise and glory for it was God that spoke to me to write "THE BREATH OF GOD" God is the one who gives breath to you and me and to our children.

These are the words I will stand on until the day my Lord calls me home!

2 Corinthians 12: 9, 10 MY GRACE IS SUFFIENT FOR YOU, FOR MY POWER IS MADE PERFECT IN WEAKNESS.

Therefore I will boast all the more gladly about my weaknesses, so that Christ power may rest on me. That is why, for Christ sake. I delight in weaknesses, in insults, in hardships, in persecutions, in difficulties. For when I am weak, then I am strong.

PRAISE BE TO GOD!

CPSIA information can be obtained at www.ICGtesting.com
Printed in the USA
266853BV00001B/8/P